Things to Know Before Starting or Investing in a P2P Fashion Rental Platform

First published by Kjøller 2023

Disclaimer:

The information contained in this book is provided for general informational purposes only. While every effort has been made to ensure that the information is accurate and up-to-date, The Author makes no representations or warranties of any kind, express or implied, about the completeness, accuracy, reliability, suitability, or availability with respect to the information, products, services, or related graphics contained in the book for any purpose.

The Author disclaims any liability for any loss or damage, including without limitation, indirect or consequential loss or damage, or any loss or damage whatsoever arising from loss of data or profits arising out of, or in connection with, the use of this book.

Readers are solely responsible for determining the appropriateness of the information contained in this book for their specific purposes and should seek professional advice before acting upon any information contained herein. The Author shall not be liable for any damages of any kind arising from the use of this book or the information contained herein.

Table of Contents

Introduction

The fashion industry is constantly evolving, and so are the ways people consume fashion. Peer-to-peer fashion rental platforms have emerged as an alternative to traditional fashion retail, offering individuals the opportunity to rent fashion items from one another. While it can provide a sustainable and cost-efficient solution for fashion enthusiasts, it involves complexities that require attention.

This glossary provides a comprehensive list of terms and their definitions that will help anyone who wants to start or invest in a P2P fashion rental platform. It covers not only the technical jargon used in such platforms but also the day-to-day operations, legal issues, and marketing strategies. Whether you are a beginner or an experienced investor, this book will equip you with the knowledge you need to navigate the P2P fashion rental industry.

Advertising

A marketing technique used to promote the platform to a wider audience. Advertising can take on different forms, such as social media ads, display ads, or influencer marketing. An effective advertising strategy increases the platform's visibility and attracts more users.

Affiliate Marketing

It is a marketing channel in which an affiliate promotes the platform through links, banners, or ads on their website or social media platforms. The affiliate earns a commission on successful referrals that result in a rental or sale of an item via the platform.

Agreement

A legal document outlining the terms and conditions for renting or lending on the platform. The agreement establishes a legal framework between the renter and the lender to protect both parties and ensure a smooth transaction.

Analytics

Analytics refers to the process of analyzing data to derive insights into the platform's performance. This data includes user behavior, item popularity, and revenue generated. The insights help the platform improve its operations and enhance the user experience.

API Integration

API stands for application programming interface. It is a tool that enables the platform to connect to third-party services, such as payment gateways or shipping services. This integration streamlines the process of renting or lending and enhances the user experience.

Arbitration

In the event of a dispute between the renter and the lender, an arbitrator can serve as a neutral third party to resolve the conflict. Platforms typically offer this service as part of their policies.

Assets

Assets refer to the items available for rent on the platform. This term applies to clothing, accessories, and other fashion-related items that users list for rent.

Authentication

This pertains to the process of verifying the identity of the user before allowing them to access the P2P Fashion Rental platform. It can be done through email, phone number, social media accounts, or any other verification method used by the platform.

Authority

It refers to the credibility or expertise of the platform or its founders in the market. High authority translates into trust and can influence the decision of users to join, rent, or lend on the platform.

Availability

It refers to the number of items available for rent on the platform at a given time. The availability of items is essential for both renters and lenders since it directly affects the success of the platform.

Back-End Operations

All the processes that happen behind the scenes to maintain a P2P fashion rental platform, such as logistics, customer support, and data management. They are essential to ensure efficient and seamless transactions for both renters and owners.

Beta Test

The phase in which a P2P fashion rental platform is tested by a group of users before its official launch. Feedback from beta testers is critical to identify and fix any bugs or user experience issues before the platform goes public.

Blockchain

A decentralized, secure digital ledger that provides transparency and immutability to P2P fashion rental platforms. Using blockchain technology can improve the authenticity of fashion items, protect users' data, and increase the efficiency of transactions.

Booking System

A feature of many P2P fashion rental platforms that allows users to reserve specific items they wish to rent. It provides pricing information, availability, and the necessary information to complete the booking process.

Borrower Agreement

A legal document that outlines the terms and conditions of the contract between the borrower and the P2P fashion rental platform. It covers issues such as rental fees, delivery arrangements, return policies, and the responsibilities of both parties.

Brand Ambassadors

Social media influencers or celebrities hired by P2P fashion rental platforms to promote their services and increase brand awareness among target audiences. Having well-known brand ambassadors can help establish trust and credibility with potential users.

Brand Authenticity

A critical factor in the P2P fashion rental industry, as users expect genuine products from recognizable brands. Platforms must ensure that all items are certified authentic by the original manufacturers or authorized distributors to maintain customer trust.

Business Model

The approach taken by a P2P fashion rental platform to make a profit. Typically, platforms charge a commission from each rental transaction, subscription fees, or advertising revenue.

Business Plan

A document that outlines the goals, strategies, and financial projections of a P2P fashion rental platform. It includes market research, competitor analysis, marketing plans, and a budget for the platform's development and ongoing operations. A comprehensive business plan is crucial for securing funding from investors and guiding the platform's growth.

Buyer Protection

A set of measures to guarantee that renters receive what they ordered, including quality assurance checks, damage insurance, and dispute resolution mechanisms. Ensuring buyer protection is critical to maintaining a good reputation and increasing market share for rental platforms.

Collaboration

A crucial aspect of a P2P fashion rental platform is collaboration between the platform, lenders, renters, and other stakeholders. This collaboration extends to seamless communication and a system for dispute resolution in case of any issues. A clear understanding of the roles and responsibilities of all parties involved should be established at the outset to minimize possible misunderstandings.

Community building

A sense of community building is critical for long-term success in the P2P fashion rental industry. A successful platform should create a welcoming and engaging user experience through user-generated content, forums, and social media integration. This community-building can foster brand loyalty, better user engagement, and overall platform growth.

Compliance

A P2P fashion rental platform must comply with all relevant legal and regulatory requirements, such as tax laws, data privacy regulations, and consumer protection laws. Failure to comply can result in legal liabilities, financial penalties, or reputational damage.

Consumer protection

One of the main challenges in the P2P fashion rental industry is ensuring consumer protection, especially since lenders on the platform are often individuals rather than established business entities. User ratings and reviews of each lender and renter can be used to encourage behavioral norms that promote responsible practices.

Contingency plan

A comprehensive contingency plan is essential before starting or investing in a P2P fashion rental platform. It should cover scenarios such as equipment failure, disputes or conflicts, and cases of fraud. The contingency plan should also outline a strategy for dealing with crises that may occur unexpectedly.

Copyright infringement

There is a risk of copyright infringement in the P2P fashion rental industry since lenders on the platform may not be the original designers of the clothes they lend. The platform must ensure that all lenders have legal or rightful ownership of the clothes they publish on the platform to avoid legal liabilities.

CRM system

A customer relationship management (CRM) system is an essential tool for any P2P fashion rental platform. It can capture user behavior, feedback, communication preferences, and other important data. This information can be used to improve user experience, reduce disputes, and enhance the platform's overall performance.

Curation

The key to standing out in the competitive P2P fashion rental industry is providing curated content that caters to user preferences. This can be achieved through AI algorithms, personalization techniques, and user feedback. Successful curation can lead to higher-quality content, low churn rates, and increased user engagement.

Customer service

Providing outstanding customer service is vital to the success of a P2P fashion rental platform. An in-house customer service team can address user concerns, respond to inquiries, and provide technical support. Providing excellent customer service can go a long way in building user trust and loyalty.

Cybersecurity

The P2P fashion rental industry is also vulnerable to cyber threats such as data breaches, hacking, and phishing attacks. The platform should implement comprehensive cybersecurity measures such as encryption, secure payment gateways, and regular audits to prevent potential risks.

Data Analytics

A process through which raw data is collected, analyzed and interpreted to gain insights and make informed decisions. In a P2P Fashion Rental platform context, data analytics can be used to determine customer preferences, popular items and pricing strategies. Analytics tools can also be used to optimize operations like inventory management and logistics.

Data Privacy

The protection of sensitive or personal data collected by an organization. In the context of a P2P Fashion Rental platform, data privacy is crucial to maintaining customer trust and can involve measures like encryption, secure user authentication, and strict data access policies.

Database Management

The process of organizing, storing, and securing data in a structured manner. In a P2P Fashion Rental platform context, effective database management can lead to optimized user experiences, improved performance, and better security.

Decentralized Platform

A platform that operates on a distributed network rather than centralized servers. In the context of a P2P Fashion Rental platform, a decentralized platform can offer numerous benefits like improved security, lower costs, and improved flexibility.

Demand Forecasting

The process of estimating the amount of future demand for a product or service by analyzing past trends and data. In the context of a P2P Fashion Rental platform, accurate demand forecasting can lead to improvements in inventory management, pricing, and marketing strategies.

Digital Identity Verification

The process of verifying the identity of a user through various digital means like biometrics, government-issued IDs and other authentication measures. In a P2P Fashion Rental platform context, digital identity verification can help mitigate risks related to fraud, identity theft, and other illegal activities.

Digital Marketing

The use of digital channels such as social media, search engines, and email to promote products or services. In a P2P Fashion Rental platform context, digital marketing can be used to attract new customers, increase brand awareness and promote special offers.

Dispute Resolution

A process designed to resolve conflicts or disagreements between parties in a constructive and fair manner. In a P2P Fashion Rental platform context, dispute resolution may involve resolving issues related to damaged or lost items, late returns, or conflicts over pricing.

Double-Sided Platform

A platform that connects multiple parties on both sides of a market. In the context of a P2P Fashion Rental platform, a double-sided platform connects renters and lenders, providing benefits like increased inventory and better pricing options.

Dynamic Pricing

A pricing strategy where prices for goods or services change in real-time based on various factors like supply and demand, customer preferences and market trends. In the context of a P2P Fashion Rental platform, dynamic pricing can help optimize revenue by adjusting prices to match supply and demand.

Easy-to-Use Interface/Platform

An intuitive user interface that makes it easy for users to navigate and successfully rent or lend fashion items. An easy to use system reduces the burden on users and promotes repeat users.

Efficient Inventory Management

A system that tracks the lender's inventory and ensures the availability of rental items. The inventory management system allows users to view and rent available fashion items quickly.

Electronic Signature

A legally binding digital signature used to confirm agreement to the rental agreement terms and conditions. This feature streamline the agreement process and helps build trust between users.

Embedding a Payment Gateway

The process of integrating a secure payment system into the platform to facilitate transactions. It's necessary to have a robust and secure payment gateway to guarantee user's financial information is secure.

Endorsement System

An algorithm or program that allows users to rate and review their experience with each other. This feature is vital for P2P fashion rental platforms to establish trust and credibility between users who do not know each other.

End-to-End Encryption

A security mechanism that encrypts data and communication between lenders and borrowers. End-to-end encryption ensures secure communication between users protecting sensitive information during transactions.

Escrow Service

A third-party platform that holds funds from both parties until the transaction is complete. In the case of a P2P fashion rental platform, both the lender and borrower deposit their funds into escrow until the rented item is returned, ensuring the security of the transaction for both parties.

Excess Wear and Tear

Refers to the damage or wear on the item beyond ordinary use. This can include stains, rips, and other damages. It's important to outline this in the rental agreement and to set specific guidelines for any additional charges or penalties.

Execution of the Rental Agreement

The finalized agreement between lender and borrower that outlines the terms and conditions of the rental, including rental dates, fees, and insurance requirements. It's essential to detail the agreement to ensure a smooth rental process.

Experience

A user's experience renting or lending an item on the P2P fashion rental platform. This includes the ease of use, quality of communication, and overall satisfaction. Ensuring a positive user experience can promote repeat users and positive endorsements.

Fashion Rental Platform

A P2P (peer-to-peer) platform that allows users to rent fashion items to one another. It differs from traditional fashion retail in that the items available for rent are typically high-end or designer pieces, and are owned and supplied by individual users rather than by the platform itself.

Fashion seasonality

The cyclical nature of fashion trends and the corresponding demand for certain types of clothing at different times of year. Understanding fashion seasonality is important for a P2P fashion rental platform as it can impact the types of items available for rent and the pricing of those items.

Fashion trends

The current and anticipated styles and tendencies in the fashion world. Understanding fashion trends is important for a P2P fashion rental platform as it helps ensure that the items available for rent are in demand and likely to be rented.

Feedback and ratings

A feature that allows users to rate and review their experiences renting or lending items on the platform. This can be a valuable tool for building trust between users and ensuring that high-quality items and services are being offered.

Fees

The charges levied by the platform for using its services. This may include a commission on rentals, transaction fees, or other charges.

Fixed-price vs. auction-based rental

The two main models for pricing rentals on a P2P fashion rental platform. The fixed-price model sets a specific price for each item, while the auction-based model allows users to bid on items and negotiate a rental price.

Franchise

A business model in which an existing company grants the right to use its name and business model to independent operators. A P2P fashion rental platform may choose to operate as a franchise in order to expand its reach and increase its user base.

Fraud prevention

Measures taken by the platform to prevent fraud, such as verifying the identities of users, implementing secure payment systems, and monitoring transactions for suspicious activity.

Fulfillment

The process of managing orders and shipping products to customers. In the context of a P2P fashion rental platform, fulfillment would involve coordinating the rental of an item between the owner and the renter, ensuring that the item is delivered on time and in good condition, and handling any returns or disputes that may arise.

Funding

The financial resources needed to start and grow a P2P fashion rental platform. This may include investments from venture capitalists or other sources, as well as revenue generated from rentals and other fees.

Gamification

The incorporation of game elements into non-game contexts, such as a P2P fashion rental platform. Gamification can enhance user engagement and motivation by creating a sense of competition or achievement through features such as badges, leaderboards, and rewards.

GDPR compliance

The adherence to the General Data Protection Regulation, a set of laws designed to protect the privacy and rights of EU citizens with regards to their personal data. P2P fashion rental platforms that operate in the EU are required to comply with GDPR regulations, which can impact their data collection, processing, and storage practices.

Geo-targeting

The practice of delivering advertising or other content to users based on their geographic location. P2P fashion rental platforms can use geo-targeting to tailor their marketing messages or product offerings to specific regions or cities where there is high demand for fashion rentals.

Gig economy

A labor market characterized by short-term contracts or freelance work rather than permanent jobs. P2P fashion rental platforms can be seen as part of the gig economy, as they allow individuals to monetize their underutilized assets (such as clothing) on a part-time basis.

Globalization

The integration of markets and economies around the world that has led to increased trade and the rise of multinational corporations. This has created opportunities for P2P fashion rental platforms to expand their reach and offer international shipping, allowing users to access a wider range of clothing options from around the world.

Group buying

A purchasing strategy in which multiple buyers come together to buy a product or service in bulk, often at a discounted price. P2P fashion rental platforms can leverage group buying to negotiate better rates from suppliers or encourage users to make larger orders.

Growth hacking

A marketing technique that focuses on rapid experimentation across channels and product development to identify the most effective ways to grow a business. P2P fashion rental platforms can use growth hacking to test different strategies for acquiring new users and retaining existing ones, such as referral programs and social media advertising.

Growth potential

The potential for a business or market to expand and increase its revenue over time. The growth potential of a P2P fashion rental platform will depend on factors such as the size of the market, the level of competition, and the platform's ability to attract and retain users.

Guaranteed returns

A feature offered by some P2P fashion rental platforms that guarantees a certain level of revenue for users who lend out their clothing items. This can provide a sense of security for lenders who are concerned about the potential risks of providing their clothes to strangers.

Guarantor

A third party that provides a guarantee or safety net for transactions on a P2P fashion rental platform. This can take the form of insurance, escrow services, or dispute resolution mechanisms to protect users from fraud or financial losses.

Hauler

A Hauler is an influencer or blogger who has a significant following on social media and is interested in partnering with P2P fashion rental platforms. Haulers promote the platform and its services to their followers in exchange for free rentals or compensation.

Host Fee

The Host Fee is the percentage of the rental price that is charged by the P2P fashion rental platform to the lender. The Host Fee helps to cover the costs of running and maintaining the platform. Host Fees vary between platforms and can range from 10% to 25% of the rental price.

Image recognition

Image recognition technology is used to help customers find the specific rental items they are looking for on the P2P Fashion Rental platform. It reduces the search time for users and makes their search more accurate and convenient. The platform can use artificial intelligence (AI) to improve image recognition technology, making it more accurate and efficient.

In-app messaging

In-app messaging is a feature that allows users to communicate with each other during the rental process. It is crucial for users to send messages and questions to each other to clarify any doubts or misunderstandings. This feature also provides an opportunity for feedback and ratings after the rental process is complete.

Incentives

Incentives refer to the rewards or benefits given to platform users to engage and bring value to the platform. These could be in the form of discounts, cashbacks, referral bonuses, or loyalty programs, among others. The incentives should be attractive enough to encourage user engagement and retention.

Income distribution

P2P Fashion Rental platforms need a mechanism to distribute the rental income between the platform and item owners. A fair and transparent revenue sharing model will ensure that both platform owners and item owners benefit from the rental process. The revenue sharing model should be communicated clearly to both parties and should be easy to understand.

Insurance

Insurance refers to the coverage for damage, loss, or theft of rental items on the P2P Fashion Rental platform. It is crucial for the platform to have an insurance policy that covers both the owners and renters of rental items. This coverage will provide protection against any potential mishaps during the rental process.

Integration

Integration is the process of connecting different systems and technologies on the P2P Fashion Rental platform. It enables different users to connect efficiently, for example, users can use their social media profiles or other online authentication processes to access the platform. The more integrated the platform is, the easier it will be for users to access and enjoy the platform's services.

Interface

The interface is the part of the P2P Fashion Rental platform that users interact with to browse and rent items. The interface should be user-friendly, easy to navigate, and visually appealing to attract new users. Its design, colors, and layout should be consistent across all pages to provide a seamless user experience.

Internationalization

The P2P Fashion Rental platform should have the ability to cater to users in different regions and countries worldwide. This means that the platform needs to be sensitive to different cultures, languages, currencies, and legal requirements. Internationalization increases the platform's user base and can lead to more revenue.

Inventory

This term refers to the list of products or items that are available on the P2P Fashion Rental platform for rent. The platform should have updated and accurate inventory data to show what is available for customers to rent. The inventory should be well-organized, and have detailed descriptions, such as size, color, and condition to avoid any misunderstandings.

Item categories

The P2P Fashion Rental platform should have different categories of items that can be rented. These categories include clothing, accessories, shoes, bags, and many more. Offering a wide range of item categories will attract a broader range of users since it caters to different market segments.

Jargon

This term refers to the specialized language and terminology used within a specific field or industry. For a P2P fashion rental platform, jargon may include technical terms related to web development, legal terminology related to liability and insurance, and fashion industry terminology related to clothing styles and trends. It is important for users and investors in the platform to understand relevant jargon in order to communicate effectively and make informed decisions.

Java

This term refers to a programming language that is commonly used for developing web applications, among other uses. In the context of a P2P fashion rental platform, Java can be used to create and maintain the backend infrastructure of the platform, including databases and server applications. This can help ensure the reliability and scalability of the platform, while also improving data security.

Javascript

This term refers to a programming language often used to create interactive and dynamic elements on websites. For a P2P fashion rental platform, Javascript can be used to create features such as search filters, item previews, and user reviews. These interactive tools can help improve the user experience and encourage more engagement on the platform.

JavaScript Frameworks

This term refers to libraries of pre-written code that utilize the JavaScript programming language to develop dynamic and interactive web applications. JavaScript frameworks can be used on a P2P fashion rental platform to create advanced features such as chat functions, payment processing, and item recommendations. Implementing these frameworks can help enhance the functionality and user experience of the platform, while also streamlining the development process for developers.

Joint liability

This term refers to the shared responsibility among multiple parties for any damages, losses, or legal issues that may arise from using a P2P fashion rental platform. As individuals rent out their personal clothing items to others, there is a risk of damage or loss. However, if the platform enforces joint liability, each user is accountable for their own actions and any harm caused to others. This can help ensure fair compensation and protect the reputation of the platform.

JOMO

This term stands for "Joy Of Missing Out" and refers to the idea of enjoying time spent alone or away from social obligations. In the context of a P2P fashion rental platform, JOMO can be experienced by users who no longer feel the pressure to constantly buy expensive clothing items in order to keep up with social expectations. Instead, they can enjoy the convenience and affordability of renting items on the platform, while still feeling stylish and fashionable.

JSON

This term stands for "JavaScript Object Notation" and refers to a lightweight data interchange format that is commonly used for web applications. JSON can be used on a P2P fashion rental platform to transmit and store information such as user profiles, item listings, and transaction data. This can help improve the efficiency and reliability of the platform, while also providing a more seamless user experience.

Judgment

This term refers to the final decision made by a court of law or arbitrator in a legal dispute. For a P2P fashion rental platform, judgments may come into play in the event of legal issues arising between users, such as disputes over damages or unpaid fees. It is important for the platform to have a clear and fair judgment process in place to resolve such disputes and maintain the trust of its users.

Jurisdiction

This term refers to the geographic area where legal authority applies. For a P2P fashion rental platform, jurisdiction is important to consider because different laws and regulations may apply based on the location of the platform, its users, and the rented items. It is important to understand and comply with applicable laws to ensure legal protection and prevent any liabilities or disputes.

Juxtaposition

This term refers to the placement of two contrasting elements side-by-side in order to emphasize their differences. In the context of a P2P fashion rental platform, juxtaposition can be seen in the contrast between high-end designer clothing being offered alongside affordable fast-fashion pieces. This technique can be used to attract a wider range of customers with different tastes and budgets, while also setting the platform apart from traditional rental services.

Key Performance Indicators (KPIs)

KPIs are essential metrics for P2P fashion rental platforms as they help to measure the platform's success and growth. KPIs can include metrics such as the number of active users, conversion rates, revenue, and customer satisfaction levels. P2P fashion rental platforms need to track KPIs consistently to analyze their business performance and make adjustments, making data-driven decisions to increase the platform's profitability.

K-factor

The K-factor is a metric used to measure the growth and virality of P2P fashion rental platforms. It is a ratio that measures the number of new users recruited by existing users. The K-factor is essential for P2P fashion rental platforms because it shows how efficiently the platform can grow and the sustainability of the business model. A higher K-factor typically indicates a more profitable and scalable business.

Knowledge Base

A knowledge base is an essential resource for users of P2P fashion rental platforms. It is a centralized repository of information and advice on how to use the platform, how to navigate the website, and how to address common issues that may arise. Knowledge bases can be in the form of FAQ pages, tutorials, videos, and other resources that help users get the most out of the platform. A comprehensive knowledge base can also help reduce customer support requests.

KYC

KYC stands for Know Your Customer, which is an important process for P2P fashion rental platforms to verify the identity of their users. This term involves collecting personal information and documents from users to ensure that they are trustworthy and not engaging in any fraudulent activities. The KYC process includes verifying the user's name, address, contact information, and payment information. P2P fashion rental platforms use KYC to protect their users and maintain a safe and secure online marketplace.

Late fee

A penalty fee charged by a P2P fashion rental platform when a renter fails to return an item on time. Late fees are typically charged on a per day or per hour basis, depending on the platform's policy.

Legal fees

The costs of obtaining legal advice and support if disputes arise between renters and lenders. This can be an important cost to consider when starting or investing in a P2P fashion rental platform.

Lender

A person who rents out a fashion item through a P2P fashion rental platform.

Lessee

A person who rents a fashion item from a lender via a P2P fashion rental platform.

Liability insurance

Insurance coverage provided by a P2P fashion rental platform to protect renters and owners from any damage or loss to rented items. This insurance typically covers accidental damage, theft or loss of the rented item.

Limited liability

The legal principle that limits an owner's potential financial losses to the amount they have invested in the rental transaction.

Listing fee

A fee charged by a P2P fashion rental platform when a member lists an item for rent on the platform. Typically, this fee is a percentage of the rental fee charged by the owner of the item.

Location tracking

The use of technology to track the movement of rented items, ensuring that renters return items to the correct location and at the right time.

Logistics

The process of managing the movement of rented items from the owner to the renter and back again. This includes shipping, handling, and delivery logistics.

Loss of use fee

A fee charged by a P2P fashion rental platform when an item is damaged or lost while on rent, to compensate the owner for lost rental income while the item is being replaced or repaired.

Maintenance

Maintenance is a critical aspect of a P2P fashion rental platform. Keeping the fashion items in excellent condition is essential to attract and retain customers.

Management Information Systems (MIS)

MIS plays a vital role in the operations of a P2P fashion rental platform. They are responsible for managing communications, payments, inventory, and rating systems.

Margins

Refers to the difference between the rental and buying price of the fashion items. It is how the platform earns money from each transaction.

Marketing Strategies

The approach taken by the platform to promote itself in the market. This includes branding, advertising, social media promotions, etc. An effective marketing strategy is crucial to attract and retain customers.

Marketplace-to-Consumer (M2C)

A platform where individuals can rent fashion items to consumers directly. This eliminates the need for a middleman, making the process more cost-effective for the renters.

Merits and Demerits

Both advantages and disadvantages are significant in a P2P fashion rental business. It is crucial to weigh them out to make informed investment decisions.

Minimum order value (MOV)

The minimum amount that a borrower needs to spend on a fashion rental. It is set by the platform and usually considered to avoid the cost of multiple small transactions.

Monitoring

One of the critical functions of a P2P fashion rental platform is monitoring what is being rented out and returned. It ensures that borrowers and lenders are accountable and transparent in their transactions, thereby building trust between the parties involved.

Multi-sided platform

A platform that provides a service to both the supply and demand side of the market. In the P2P fashion rental context, it connects borrowers with lenders by taking a percentage of the transaction.

Mutual Trust

A fundamental aspect of a P2P rental platform, as it promotes a sense of reliability and dependability between borrowers and lenders. It is essential to generate a good reputation for both parties.

Nationality restrictions

Limitations placed by a platform on the countries or regions from where users can access the services or become members.

NDA

Non-Disclosure Agreement (NDA) is a legal document that outlines the confidential information that a party wants to protect and limit access to. In the case of a P2P Fashion Rental platform, NDAs could be used to protect user data or intellectual property.

Net Promoter Score (NPS)

A metric that measures customer satisfaction and loyalty by asking respondents a single question

Network effects

When a platform's value grows as the number of active users increases, creating a positive feedback loop. In a P2P Fashion Rental platform, this would mean that the more items available for rent, the more attractive the platform becomes for potential renters.

Neutrality

A concept that emphasizes the platform's role as a facilitator and not an active participant in transactions between renters and lenders. Neutrality ensures that the platform does not take sides or favor one user over the other.

NFC tags

Near Field Communication (NFC) tags are small chips that are embedded into clothing items to track their usage and keep an inventory of rental transactions.

Niche Market

A specific segment of the market that caters to a particular type of client or product. In the case of a P2P Fashion Rental platform, it would refer to the specific target audience the platform serves.

Node.js

A JavaScript runtime environment that allows developers to build scalable and high-performance applications. Node.js would be used to create the backend of a P2P Fashion Rental platform, to manage transactions and user data.

Non-compete clause

A contractual agreement between the platform and its users that prohibits users from competing with the platform by setting up similar services or businesses within a certain time frame or geographic area. In the context of P2P Fashion Rental platforms, Non-compete clauses could be used to prevent users from becoming direct competitors or creating copycat platforms.

Non-monetary compensation

A reward or benefit that is not in the form of cash. It could include things like access to exclusive events, priority reservations, or personalized styling advice in the context of a P2P Fashion Rental platform.

Offline Verification

Many P2P fashion rental platforms require renters to provide identification documents or a small deposit to ensure they are who they say they are. This is known as offline verification and is an essential process to maintain platform safety.

Onboarding Process

The process of signing up a new user onto the platform. This process may include identity verification, creating a user profile, and linking a payment method. User onboarding is crucial for platform success as it affects user experience.

On-Demand Logistics

An essential aspect of P2P fashion rental platforms is prompt and reliable delivery and pickup of rental items. On-demand logistics refers to the process of collecting, delivering, and returning items to renters as quickly as possible.

Open Listing

A rental listing that is available to all eligible renters on the platform. This means that anyone can rent the item for the specified duration and pay the stated price.

Operating Agreement

A legal document that outlines the terms and conditions of how the P2P fashion rental platform operates. It clarifies the roles and responsibilities of the owner, renters, and the platform itself, acting as a guideline for how transactions should occur. Investors should review the operating agreement before investing to avoid any unforeseen legal issues.

Operational Costs

The expenses needed to run and maintain the P2P fashion rental platform. These include marketing, customer service, server maintenance, and other operating expenses. Investors need to be aware of these expenses when assessing the profitability of the platform.

Organic Traffic

Visitors who come to the P2P fashion rental platform by typing in the website or finding it through a search engine rather than paid advertising. High organic traffic is essential for platform success to increase awareness and the potential customer base.

Outfit Curation

Selecting and curating relevant outfit choices for renters based on their preferences and style. Such personalization creates a better user experience and leads to higher customer satisfaction and customer retention.

Owner Commission

The percentage of the rental fee that goes to the platform owner. Before investing, it is crucial to determine how much the platform owner keeps out of the transaction to determine if it is a good investment opportunity.

Ownership Transfer

Ownership transfer happens when a user puts their item up for rental, and the platform takes ownership of the item for as long as it is rented through their platform. This ensures that the item is looked after and covered under the platform's insurance policy while they're in transport or in possession of the renter.

Payment gateway

A term commonly used to describe the platform's system that facilitates online transactions between two or more parties. The payment gateway on P2P fashion rental platforms handles credit card payments, transactions between renters, and owners of clothes.

Peer review system

A system in which users of P2P fashion rental platforms can rate and review other users. This system helps build trust and transparency between users and is a vital feature for any P2P platform. Peer review systems make it easier for users to decide whether to rent from or lend to a particular user on the platform.

Peer-to-peer insurance

A type of insurance policy in which users of P2P fashion rental platforms can insure their clothes and other items against damage, loss, or theft. P2P insurance policies are much cheaper than traditional insurance policies and often provide better coverage. Peer-to-peer insurance policies are also usually more flexible, as they can be custom-tailored to specific items or users on a case-by-case basis.

Peer-to-peer network

A type of network that allows individuals to share resources, knowledge, and skills without the need for a centralized authority. In the context of P2P fashion rental platforms, a peer-to-peer network connects renters with other renters or owners of clothes, so they can rent or borrow clothes from each other.

Platform monetization

The process of generating revenue from a platform in exchange for its services. P2P fashion rental platforms usually generate revenue through commission fees imposed on transactions between renters and owners of clothes. The commission fee varies from one platform to another and is often calculated as a percentage of the transaction value.

Platform-agnostic

A term that refers to a feature of P2P fashion rental platforms that allows users to access the platform from any device or web browser. A platform-agnostic platform has no restrictions or preferences for operating systems, devices, or web browsers. This feature is beneficial for users who want to access the platform from any device they have access to, without having to worry about compatibility or technical issues.

Price optimization

The process of adjusting rental prices according to supply and demand dynamics in specific locations, at specific times, or for specific clothes. Platforms can use data like traffic and sales trends to determine the best rental prices for each item in different geographies, at different times of the year, or for different types of clothes.

Privacy policies

A set of guidelines regarding how platforms handle user data, store it, and share it with third-party service providers. Privacy policies in P2P fashion rental platforms are crucial to protecting users' privacy and safety.

Product categorization

The process of organizing and grouping products according to their characteristics, attributes or features. In the context of P2P fashion rental platforms, product categorization can be used to group clothes by size, style, occasion, brand, or other relevant categories.

Profit sharing model

A model where platforms share profits obtained from transactions with the platform's users. It's an excellent way to incentivize users to promote the platform's growth and attract new users. A profit sharing model could also boost user retention and enhance the platform's reputation.

Quality control

The process of ensuring that the items rented through a P2P fashion rental platform meet the agreed-upon quality standards. This may involve inspecting items before they are listed, checking for damage or wear and tear after they are returned, and enforcing penalties for users who repeatedly return items that do not meet the agreed-upon quality standards.

Quality guarantees

Promises made by the platform operator to ensure that users are satisfied with their rentals. Quality guarantees may involve refunding or providing compensation for rentals that do not meet certain quality standards, or providing protection against fraud or misrepresentation.

Quantity limits

The maximum number of items that users are allowed to rent at a given time. Quantity limits may be set to prevent users from monopolizing popular items or to ensure that users are able to reasonably use the items they rent within the rental period.

Quarantine periods

The amount of time that items must be held in isolation between rentals to prevent the spread of disease or other contaminants. Quarantine periods may vary depending on the type of item being rented and the nature of the rental platform.

Quarterly reports

Regular reports that summarize key metrics and performance indicators for the platform over a given quarter. Quarterly reports may be used to track the success of the platform and identify areas for improvement, as well as to provide transparency to investors and other stakeholders.

Quasi-insurance

Insurance-like protections that may be offered by the rental platform to protect users against loss or damage to rented items. Quasi-insurance may not offer the same level of protection as traditional insurance policies, but may still provide users with valuable peace of mind when renting high-value items.

Queue management

The process of managing user requests in a fair and efficient way. This may involve prioritizing requests based on factors such as user ratings or how frequently they use the platform, as well as implementing systems to prevent users from monopolizing popular items or flooding the platform with excessive requests.

Quick payments

A payment system that allows users to quickly and easily pay for rentals without having to go through a lengthy checkout process. Quick payment systems may use stored payment information or other methods to streamline the payment process.

Quick response times

The speed with which the platform responds to user requests, inquiries, and complaints. Quick response times are important for maintaining user satisfaction and confidence, as well as for resolving issues before they escalate into more serious problems. Platforms may use automated systems, staff training, or other strategies to improve their response times.

Quota systems

A system that limits the number of users who are allowed to use the platform or rent particular items. Quota systems may be used to manage demand or to ensure that the platform is able to effectively manage the inventory of items that are available for rent.

Relevant Market

The target audience and customer base for the P2P Fashion Rental platform, including demographics, lifestyle, and socioeconomic status. Understanding the relevant market is crucial in developing an effective marketing strategy and ensuring the platform's success.

Rental Agreement

The legal contract between the lender and renter outlining the terms and conditions of the rental, including payment, delivery, and return policies.

Rental Fee

The amount that the renter pays to borrow the garment.

Rental Period

The length of time that the renter can keep the garment before returning it to the lender.

Renting Limitations

The restrictions on rental, which can include limitations on the size or type of garments available for rent, geographic locations, and user age or experience requirements.

Reputation Management

The process of monitoring, influencing, and controlling a platform's online reputation. It involves monitoring customer reviews, social media comments, and responding to negative feedback to ensure that the platform is perceived positively by potential users and investors.

Return Policy

The guidelines and rules regarding how and when items must be returned, including any late fees or penalties.

Returns Management

The system that enables P2P Fashion Rental platforms to manage the handling of returned garments, including inspection, cleaning, restocking, and re-listing on the platform.

Revenue Model

The business model that the P2P Fashion Rental platform will adopt to generate income, which can include subscription fees, transaction fees, and commissions on sales.

Risk Management

The process of identifying, assessing, and mitigating potential risks associated with the P2P Fashion Rental platform, including financial risks, data security risks, legal risks, and reputational risks.

Scalability

Scalability is the ability of a business to grow and adapt to increasing demand while maintaining performance and quality. P2P fashion rental platforms need to be scalable in order to be successful. They must be able to handle larger volumes of users and clothing inventory while ensuring quality services, faster delivery, and lower costs. It's also crucial to have scalability in marketing, customer service, and supply chain management to maintain high-quality services.

Seasonality

Seasonality, in the context of P2P fashion rental platforms, refers to the fluctuation of demand and supply of fashion rentals during different seasons. For example, high demand for coats in winter and swimsuits in summer. Seasonal changes influence the type of clothing that platforms need to have in their inventory, their pricing strategy, and marketing techniques. Seasonality can also impact the duration of rental periods and how often users rent certain types of clothing.

Security

Security refers to the measures and mechanisms put in place to protect a business's data, user information, and financial transactions. P2P fashion rental platforms must ensure that user data is accurately stored and protected through encrypted systems, efficient authentication processes, and regular cybersecurity checks. Moreover, platforms must put in place systems to handle fraudulent activities, disputes, and identify theft. Security breaches can have severe legal and reputational consequences that may affect the platform's credibility, branding, and user retention.

Sharing Economy

The sharing economy refers to a business model based on shared use or access of resources. P2P fashion rental platforms operate using a sharing economy model, where users can rent out or borrow clothing instead of buying them. The sharing economy is a sustainable alternative to traditional consumerism that focuses on reducing waste and promoting community sharing of resources. This model also emphasizes the importance of environmental conservation, and social and economic empowerment through resource sharing.

Smart Contracts

Smart contracts are self-executing digital contracts that automate the exchange of data and minimize the need for intermediary parties (such as lawyers). P2P fashion rental platforms use smart contracts to establish legal agreements between the lender and the borrower. They work using blockchain technology, which centralizes and secures all records while excluding third-party entities. Smart contracts make the rental process quicker, more transparent, cheaper, and less prone to human error and fraud.

Social Media Marketing

Social media marketing refers to brand promotion through social media platforms such as Facebook, Twitter, Instagram, and LinkedIn. P2P fashion rental platforms use social media marketing to reach their target consumers and increase user engagement. Social media marketing provides the means to communicate directly with users, showcase their services' benefits, and collect feedback. Platforms can also use social media to run promotional campaigns, launch new features or products, and encourage users to share their rental experience.

Subscribers

Subscribers are individuals who have signed up for a subscription service, such as a P2P fashion rental platform. Subscribers are the primary target market of these platforms and are the people who will use the service to rent clothes or accessories. It's important to have a solid subscriber base to establish revenue streams and ensure sustainable growth for the platform. Platforms focus on attracting subscribers, maximizing user retention through quality services, and building long-lasting relationships with them.

Subscription-based Model

A subscription-based model is a payment plan where users pay a fixed fee at regular intervals (weekly, monthly, yearly) to gain access to services or products. P2P fashion rental platforms operate using this model, which means they allow users to borrow clothes for a period of time in exchange for a fee paid frequently. Users pay recurring fees to rent as many garments as they like at any given time within the service's terms and conditions.

Supply Chain Management

Supply chain management is the coordination of various activities involved in getting a product or service to the end consumer. In the context of P2P fashion rental platforms, the supply chain includes every aspect of the rental process, from the initial legal agreements, the collection of garments from suppliers/vendors, to lending them to end-users, then receiving them back from the customers, and their final processing or cleaning. It's important to have a streamlined and efficient supply chain management system to provide quality, timely, and cost-effective rental services.

Sustainability

Sustainability refers to the ability of a business or product to operate in ways that maintain an ecological balance and meet the social and economic needs of the current and future generations. P2P fashion rental platforms contribute to sustainability by reducing the amount of clothing waste, promoting circular economy principles, and reducing demand for new clothes. In addition to that, sustainable practices such as using eco-friendly materials, ethical garment sourcing, and reducing carbon footprint, are essential for P2P fashion rental platforms to promote their sustainability agenda and create a positive impact on society and the environment.

Target market

Identifying and targeting the ideal market is important for the success of a P2P fashion rental platform. Understanding the target audience's needs, preferences, and behaviors can guide marketing efforts that can attract the right lenders and renters to the platform.

Technology

Technology infrastructure is an essential component of P2P fashion rental platforms. Deciding on the right technology stack can affect the platform's scalability, security, and user experience. Potential investors in P2P fashion rental platforms should consider the platform's technology when evaluating investment opportunities.

Terms and conditions

The terms and conditions define the rules and regulations of a P2P fashion rental platform. It outlines the responsibilities of both lenders and renters, governing rental periods, returns, damages, and cancellations. Before signing up for a P2P fashion rental platform, it is important to review and understand these terms and conditions to avoid any potential issues down the line.

Time commitment

Starting or investing in a P2P fashion rental platform requires a significant time commitment. Running a successful platform involves various tasks such as marketing, customer service, and platform maintenance. Investors should be prepared to dedicate time and resources to the platform to ensure its success.

Timing

Timing is an essential factor when starting or investing in a P2P fashion rental platform. It involves considering market trends and identifying the right opportunity to launch. It's important to launch your platform at the right time to ensure user engagement, achieve optimum growth, and attain profitability.

Transaction fee

P2P fashion rental platforms usually charge a transaction fee, which is a percentage of the total transaction amount. This fee covers costs such as payment processing, customer service, and platform maintenance. If you are planning on investing in a P2P fashion rental platform, it is essential to understand the transaction fee structure and how it will impact your investment returns.

Trust and safety

Trust and safety measures are crucial for creating a safe and secure environment. It includes measures such as ID verification, background checks, secure payment systems, and dispute resolution mechanisms. Trust and safety measures help build trust between users on the platform and can also mitigate fraudulent activity.

Trust score

A trust score is an important metric used by P2P fashion rental platforms to assess the trustworthiness of users. The score is assigned based on factors such as previous transactions, ratings, and reviews. It serves as a guideline for potential renters or lenders and helps to minimize the risk of fraudulent users on the platform.

Trust signals

Trust signals are indicators that help establish trust between potential renters and lenders on a P2P fashion rental platform. These signals include verified user badges, ratings and reviews, trust score, and secure payment systems. Trust signals help educate users about the safety and security of the platform and can encourage them to participate in rental transactions.

Trustworthy lenders

The success of P2P fashion rental platforms largely depends on the availability of trustworthy lenders. Lenders play a critical role in determining the success or failure of the platform by providing high-quality fashion pieces for renters to rent. P2P fashion rental platforms should implement measures such as verification and ratings to ensure that only trustworthy lenders can participate in rental transactions.

Underwriting process

The process of evaluating the creditworthiness of potential borrowers on the platform. For a P2P fashion rental platform that allows users to borrow high-end designer items, it is important to have a thorough underwriting process in place to reduce the risk of defaults or unpaid rentals.

Unique inventory

Refers to the selection of clothing and accessories that are available on the platform. For a P2P fashion rental platform to be successful, it is important to offer a unique selection of inventory that cannot be found elsewhere. By offering unique, designer items, the platform can attract a higher-income clientele and set itself apart from competitors.

Unique selling proposition

A unique feature or quality that sets a P2P fashion rental platform apart from its competitors. This could be anything from the selection of inventory to the ease of use of the platform. Defining and promoting the unique selling proposition is an important aspect of building brand awareness and attracting users.

Unit economics

A way of analyzing the profitability of a P2P fashion rental platform on a per-unit basis. This involves taking into account the costs of acquiring and maintaining inventory, customer acquisition costs, and operating expenses. Understanding the unit economics of a platform is important for making informed decisions about pricing and growth strategies.

Upcharging

The practice of charging fees or commissions on top of the rental price of an item. For a P2P fashion rental platform, upcharging can be a source of revenue, but it is important to keep these fees reasonable to avoid pricing users out of the platform.

User cancellation policy

The policy outlining the conditions under which a user can cancel a rental or request a refund. Clear and fair cancellation policies can help to build trust on the platform and reduce the risk of disputes between users and renters.

User engagement

The level of activity and interaction that users have with the platform. A P2P fashion rental platform can increase user engagement by providing incentives such as discounts or special promotions for frequent users, as well as creating a social media presence and hosting events.

User rating system

The system used to allow users to rate and review other users on the platform. A user rating system can allow users to build trust with each other and make more informed decisions about who they choose to rent from.

User verification

The process of verifying the identity of users on the platform. This can include verifying a user's identity through their social media accounts or requiring them to provide government-issued identification. Verifying user identities can help to build trust on the platform and reduce the risk of fraudulent activity.

User-generated content

Content that is created by users, typically photos or reviews, that can be used to promote a P2P fashion rental platform. By allowing users to post their own content, the platform can create an engaging community that can attract new users and build brand loyalty.

Validation

The process of verifying and evaluating the authenticity and quality of the clothes listed on the P2P fashion rental platform. Validation involves ensuring the accurate measurements, age, conditions, and cleanliness of clothing rentals. It also evaluates the fashion sense and the relevance of the fashion piece to the platform. Validation aims to avoid any incidence of renting unsatisfactory clothing as it can cause severe losses on the platform's reputation.

Value Proposition

The benefits or advantages that the P2P fashion rental service offers to both renters and customers. A strong value proposition can attract customers to the platform and lead to better conversion rates. It is essential to have a robust value proposition that aligns with customer needs and demands. A P2P fashion rental platform provides the opportunity to rent designer clothing and accessories for a fraction of the price available in traditional retail purchases. A robust value proposition can attract people who appreciate the benefits of a rental platform such as lower costs and sustainable practices.

Value-Add

Additional functionalities and services that are provided by P2P fashion rental platforms to add value to the rental experience. Value-Adds can consist of several elements like user reviews, styling tips, and customization options. A refinable search functionality, secure payment methods, and a user-friendly interface also serve as value-adds, allowing customers to enjoy a comprehensive online fashion rental experience.

Variation

The variety of fashion and clothing collections available on the P2P fashion rental platform. Variation is a critical aspect of any fashion platform, as it enables a broader range of customers to access the service. The ability to offer customers a wide range of fashion products and trends ensures that the platform appeals to various demographics, generating more revenue and transactions.

Vendor Management

Management of the relationships between the platform and users offering their clothes for rent. Vendor management includes activities like customer support, verification, listing quality control, and payment processing. The successful management of vendors needs to be in place to ensure smooth and consistent rental services on the platform. Platforms with favorable vendor management practices can deliver better rental experiences to the customers, resulting in positive reviews and an increase in platform reputation.

Verification

The process of checking and approving the identity of users in order to maintain safety and security on the P2P fashion rental platform. Verification can include several steps such as confirming ID documents, phone numbers, email addresses, and payment methods. It's essential to verify users before allowing them to rent clothes so that fraudulent activities can be reduced. On the other hand, if a user is renting their clothes, verification is also imperative, as it can assure safety for them too. Verification requirement ensures the authenticity of users in addition to developing trust within the P2P fashion rental community.

Verticality

The practice of focusing on a particular fashion niche or specific target market. A P2P fashion rental platform can aim to cater to specific fashion styles such as vintage clothing, streetwear, or couture. The focus on a specific fashion segment ensures that the platform can tailor its services to the specific needs or requirements of that targeted market, providing an exceptional experience.

Vigilance

The commitment of the platform to protecting its users from online fraud, cybercrime, and malicious activities. Vigilance includes the implementation of measures to monitor user activities, detection of fraudulent activities, and rapid responses to security threats. P2P fashion rental platforms are often exposed to illegal activities such as counterfeit sales, identity theft, and payment fraud. Therefore, vigilant platforms can deter these activities and provide a secure environment for its users.

Virtuous Cycle

The process of achieving continued growth on the P2P fashion rental platform by keeping the network effect in mind. The virtuous cycle begins with more customer transactions, leading to more vendors and their products being listed on the platform. This expansion leads to further customer transactions, which lead to more vendors, eventually creating a cycle of growth that continually attracts more customers and vendors. Ensuring this cycle remains virtuous is essential to achieving continued growth and success on the P2P fashion rental platform.

Visibility

The frequency of the platform's appearance on search engine results pages, social media platforms, and contextual ads. Visibility is an essential factor in any successful online business, as it can attract more customers and generate more visits to the platform. The visibility of the platform may depend on various factors such as SEO optimization, social media engagement, and the platform's promotion campaigns.

Wardrobe Management

The practice of organizing and maintaining a collection of clothing items. In a P2P fashion rental platform, it is essential to manage and keep track of the items being rented out and ensure they are in good condition for the next renter. Good management practices help to reduce the chances of loss, damage, or theft of clothing items.

Wear and Tear

The gradual damage that occurs to clothing as a result of everyday use. With P2P fashion rental, items will be regularly worn and will experience wear and tear even if renters take good care of them. It is important to anticipate such damage and make detailed photographic records of items before and after rental.

Website Design

The process of creating a website with a particular focus on layout, visual design, functionality, and user experience (UX). A well-designed website is crucial for attracting and retaining users. User-friendly features such as a responsive design and clear navigation significantly influence the success of a P2P fashion rental platform.

Wireframes

Visual guides that map out the framework and layout of a website or application. Wireframes serve as a blueprint for designing a platform and can help the designer to create a functional user interface with a good user experience.

Workflow

A chain of activities required to accomplish a specific task. In a P2P fashion rental platform, a streamlined workflow ensures that listings are uploaded in good time, renters find it easy to book items, and transactions are completed without any difficulties. A seamless workflow goes a long way in creating a positive user experience.